A B C D E F G H

I J K L M N O P

Q R S T U V X Y

Z A B C D E F G

H I J K L M N O

P Q R S T U V X

A FRENCH ALPHABET BOOK OF 1814

for Alfred Bourdier de Beauregard
created by his uncle Arnaud
at the Château de Beaumont de Beauregard

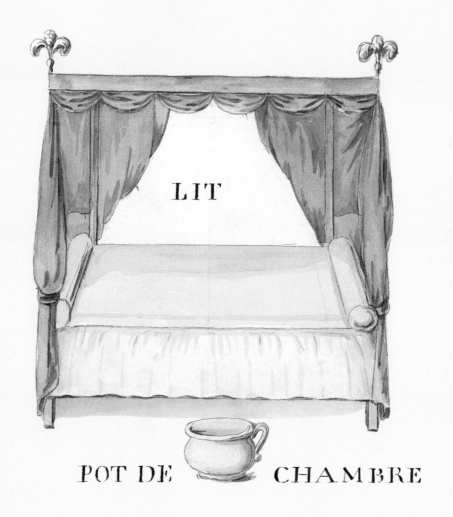

LIT

POT DE CHAMBRE

A FRENCH ALPHABET BOOK OF 1814

for Alfred Bourdier de Beauregard
created by his uncle Arnaud
at the Château de Beaumont de Beauregard

CHARLES PLANTE

RIZZOLI
NEW YORK

First published in the United States of America in 2007 by
Rizzoli International Publications, Inc.
300 Park Avenue South
New York, NY 10010
www.rizzoliusa.com

Originally published in the United Kingdom in 2004 by
Charles Plante Fine Arts
50 Gloucester Street
London SW1V 4EH
www.watercolours-drawings.com

ISBN 978-0-8478-3010-7

Library of Congress Control Number: 2007922143

2007 2008 2009 2010 / 10 9 8 7 6 5 4 3 2 1

Designed by Charles Plante
Printed and Bound in Budapest, Hungary by Folpress.

ACKNOWLEDGEMENTS
Writing, though a solitary exercise, ultimately becomes a collaborative effort.
I wish to thank especially George Manginis for the inspired translation, Victoria Frazier, Ross Fusca, James Hall,
Rev Michael Lankford, Diane Struass and Dr Rory O'Donell for his advice and attention to detail.

à Gracie, ma filleule et nièce

A French Alphabet Book of 1814

for Alfred Bourdier de Beauregard, created by his uncle Arnaud at the Château de Beaumont de Beauregard

Alberic-Alfred Bourdier de Beauregard was born in 1812, ninth child of a French aristocratic family; the early stages of his education during the second decade of the nineteenth century are succinctly represented in this original and charming series of watercolours dating from 1814, which were used as an *abécédaire*. This rare survival was beautifully hand-painted, with captioned images illustrating words spread across the *recto* of thirty-six plates, five of which with further images on the reverse, making up two-hundred and eighty-five in total. It is the work of the talented artist Arnaud (perhaps C.P. Arnaud, the author and illustrator of the *Recueil de tombeaux des quatre cimetières de Paris, avec leurs epitaphes et leurs inscriptions*, Paris *circa* 1817). Alfred, described on the manuscript as 'my nephew,' was only two years old when the drawings were created; he treasured them until his death in 1893.

Alfred's father Isaac-Gilbert was born in Pau in the Pyrenees in 1774, the son of a royal office-holder. He enrolled in the revolutionary armies between 1793 and 1795, but by 1815 he was to be a *garde-du-corps* or gentleman bodyguard to the restored King Louis XVIII. Between these momentous events he seems to have withdrawn from public life, spending his time at the Château de Beaumont de Beauregard. He thus managed to preserve his life and fortune, although the *château* was to be sold in 1818. It was there, during the month of June 1814 that the watercolours were drawn. The first one shows the *château* with its palisades, its courtyard, its ha-ha and its dovecotes (these last proudly surviving, where so many had been the first things vandalized by peasant mobs in the summer of 1789). Today the building maintains all its dependencies, and seems to underline the preservation of an aristocratic feudal world reputedly abolished in 1789 and later by the revolutionary confiscations of property of those who opposed the Revolution and went into exile as *émigrés*. It is situated near Agognes (Allier), in the Bourbonnais, itself the nursery of the Bourbon dynasty in the province of the Auvergne. First built in the fifteenth century, as it stands now it goes back to the eighteenth century, with only one round tower and the octagonal dovecote that still flanks the entrance surviving from earlier phases. The dovecote must be one of the two seen in Arnaud's drawing (and illustrated by Annie Regond, "Histoire de l'Art," in G. Rougeron *et al.*, *Bourbonnais*, Paris 1988). Unusually, all the eighteenth century annexes still exist, as well as the chapel. The *château* receives only a brief mention in Ivan Loiseau and Marcel Genermont's *Châteaux en Bourbonnais*, Paris 1961.

Alfred de Beauregard was a privileged boy whose childhood has been preserved for posterity in these water-colours, almost like that of the heroes of Alain-Fournier's *Le Grand Meaulnes*, published in 1913. It is as if the Revolution and the bewildering succession of regimes culminating in the Napoleonic Empire (1804) had been nothing but a bad dream. And indeed, by June 1814 Napoleon had been chased from his throne and King Louis XVIII was ruling France courtesy of the victorious Allies. There are clues that Arnaud was as unsure of the course of political events as any other: over the caption "flag" is shown the tricolour of the Revolution and the Napoleonic Empire flying from a flag pole crowned with the Imperial eagle clasping the wreath of victory; however, the axes of the flag are horizontally, rather than vertically, divided. By contrast, the *fleurs-de-lys* of the Royal Arms appear as a fireback and fully emblazoned under a crown on the proscenium arch of the "theatre," with the Château de Beaumont de Beauregard itself as the backdrop scene. This was evidently a family that had not rallied to the Empire; within the domain of the *château* and as far as the Beauregard family was concerned, as sort of internal rather than external *émigrés,* the exiled king never stopped ruling. This plate presents another clue or pun: the metal bathtub or "*baignoire*" is in French the same word as "theatre pit." Puns were popularised in the late eighteenth century in prints and often appeared on porcelain and other decorative arts. The little boy would read across the meaning from "theatre pit" to "bathtub," covered by the same word. Some plates obviously hide other messages, now lost to us, based on visual puns and word-play, such as that showing an open window, the heads of a child and an old man, a bow and arrow, an hour-glass and a skeleton, all moralizing, didactic comments on and symbols of the inevitable passage of time.

The images can be grouped around three or four themes: the architecture of the *château* and its annexes, of the farm-yard, village and town; the clothing proper to an aristocratic child; the furnishing of the table and kitchen, workshop and stable; and the occupations of the child, such as music, hunting, naming of animals and flowers. Some are arranged on a single plate, others are scattered across several. His braces are to be found separately from his stockings, breeches (the aristocratic *culotte*), shirt and cane; therefore, his morning dressing can be traced over many different plates. Some more emblematic designs, such as the faces showing moods and attitudes like anger and despair, were probably copied from existing encyclopaedia plates, and follow contemporary beliefs about the science of physiognomy. Similar origins and use can be assigned to the plate of the weather system, and that showing the ABC, the numbers, the clock and the sundial. Other plates are clearly intended to amuse: one shows a monument labelled "*mosolée*," with the "o" scratched out and replaced with "*au*" as in "*mausolée*." This re-spelling gives us a clue: attendant mice run up the obelisk to the triumphant cat (as the inscription on the monument is "here lies the most faithful of all cats") and the "*mausolée*" sound may suggest *miaou* in French. Other visual jokes are earthier: under the bed lies prominently a chamber pot and healthy bottom cheeks ("*cul*") crown a neat pile of "*caca*" (*i.e.* his stool in nursery language). A more sinister element of the boy's childhood is the "*martinet*" with which he could be threatened with punishment.

There is a noted absence of military uniforms and accoutrements with which an aristocratic boy would play. Only one plate shows them, whereas two highly detailed plates include esoteric ecclesiastical furnishings and this in a country which had abolished the Catholic religion in 1793-1794, and only officially re-authorized its practice in 1802. The fifteen items of church furnishings are juxtaposed with only four military images (although other items of dress or from the hunt might address this imbalance). Once again, this could be interpreted as evidence of the alienation of the French aristocracy from the Revolution and the apparently triumphant militarisation of the French State under Napoleon; on him and his signal victories this collection is strangely silent. But the watermark of the paper clearly shows the Imperial Eagle as well as the head of the Emperor, which suggests his brooding presence throughout this period.

A final clue in this series of watercolours, which abound in interesting details of architecture, lies in the plate labelled "*palais-jardin*." It shows the only other identifiable building – except from the Château de Beaumont de Beauregard – the garden front of the Tuillieries Palace in Paris, now occupied, as the Beauregard family always hoped it would be, by the restored Louis XVIII who was to rule as King of France until his death in 1824.

Charles Plante

A B C D E F G H I J K L M N O P Q R S T U V X Y Z

Cayer d'instruction

pour Alfred, Bourdier de Beauregard.

mon Neveu. 1814

Fait au Chateau de Beauregard dans le courant de Juin 1814
par Arnaud, auteur du plan en Relief de la ville de Paris

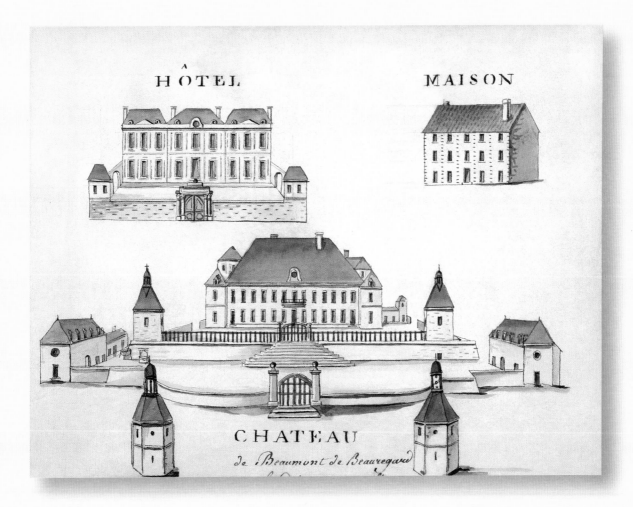

HÔTEL

MAISON

CHATEAU

de Beaumont de Beauregard

CHAUMIERE

AUBERGE

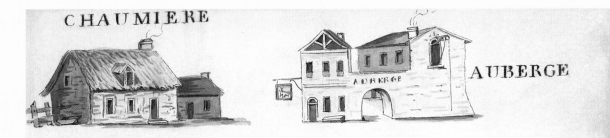

GRANGE

PRISON

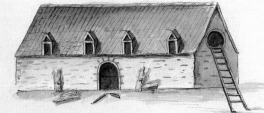

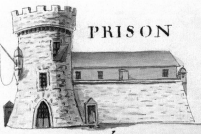

ÉCURIE

RUE

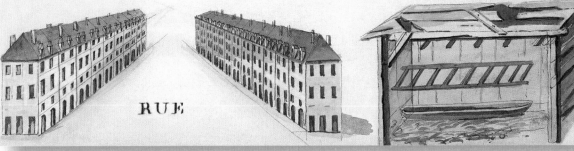

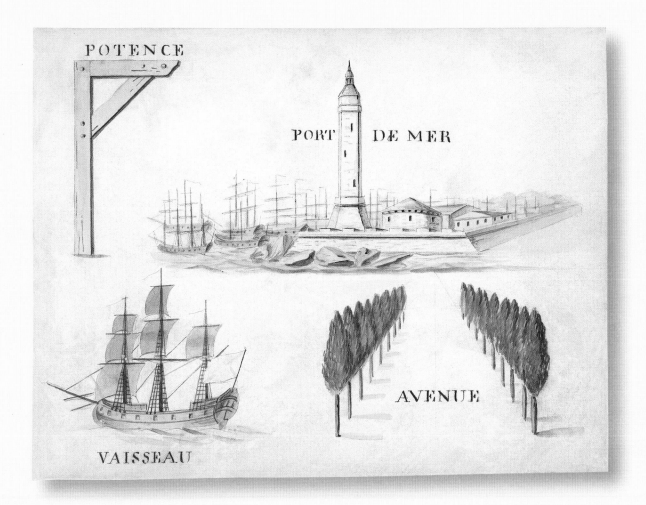

POTENCE

PORT DE MER

VAISSEAU

AVENUE

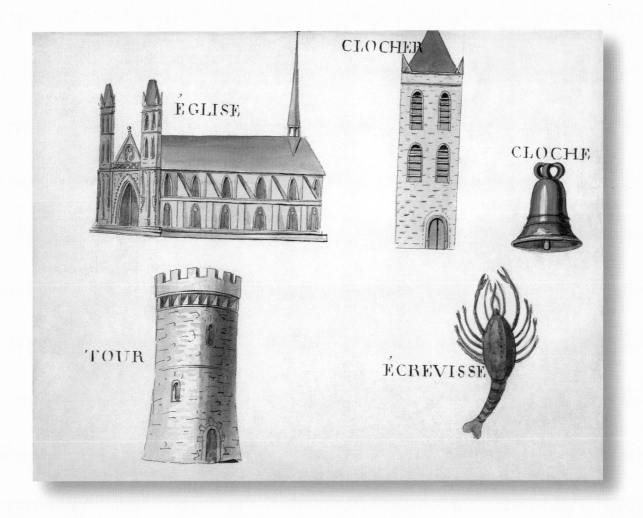

ÉGLISE

CLOCHER

CLOCHE

TOUR

ÉCREVISSE

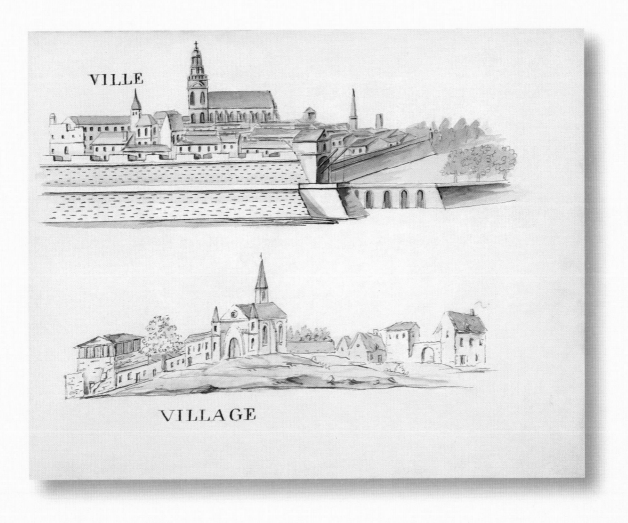

VILLE

VILLAGE

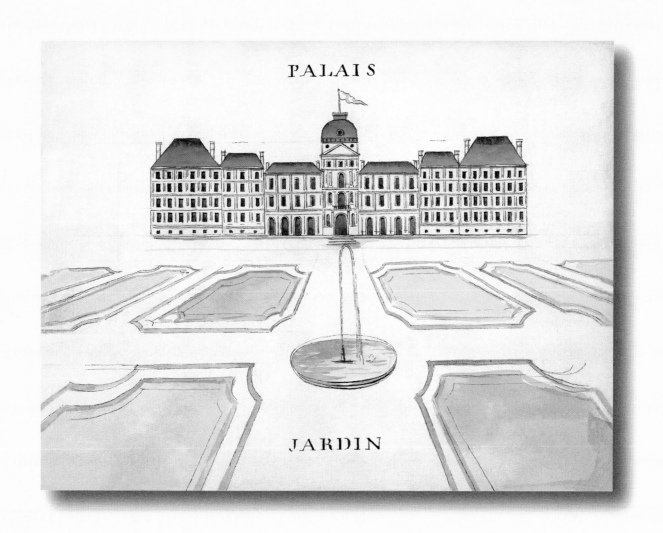

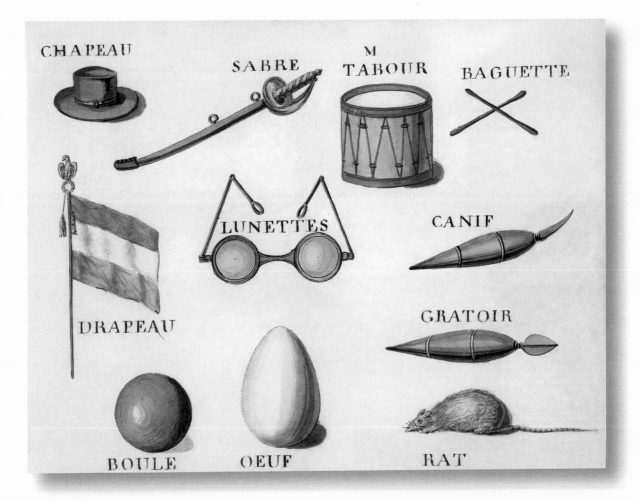

CHAPEAU

SABRE

M
TABOUR

BAGUETTE

LUNETTES

CANIF

DRAPEAU

GRATOIR

BOULE

OEUF

RAT

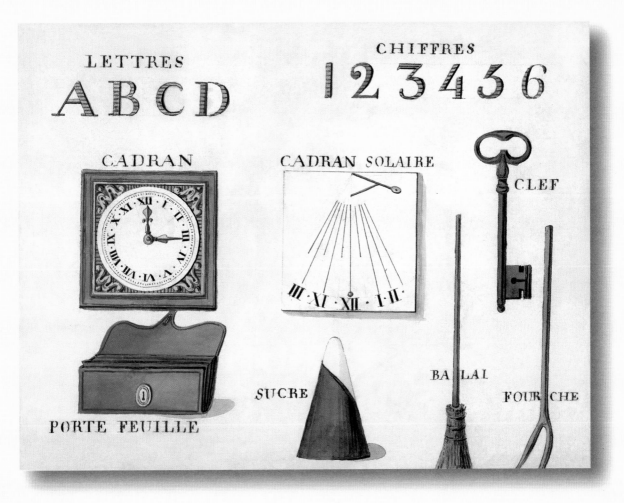

LETTRES

ABCD

CHIFFRES

123456

CADRAN

CADRAN SOLAIRE

CLEF

PORTE FEUILLE

SUCRE

BALLAI

FOURCHE

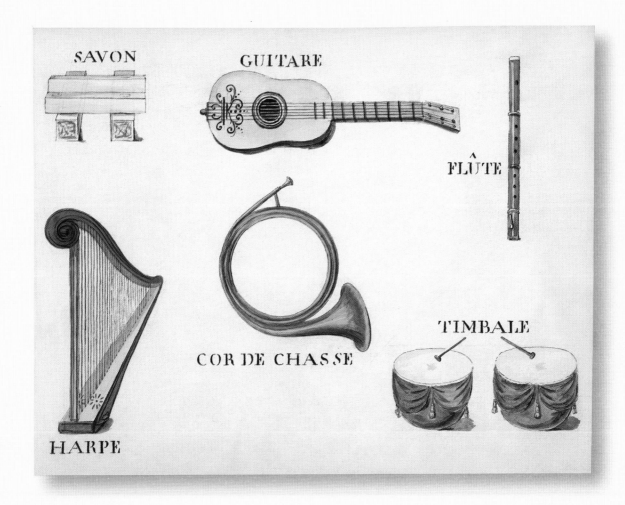

SAVON

GUITARE

FLÛTE

HARPE

COR DE CHASSE

TIMBALE

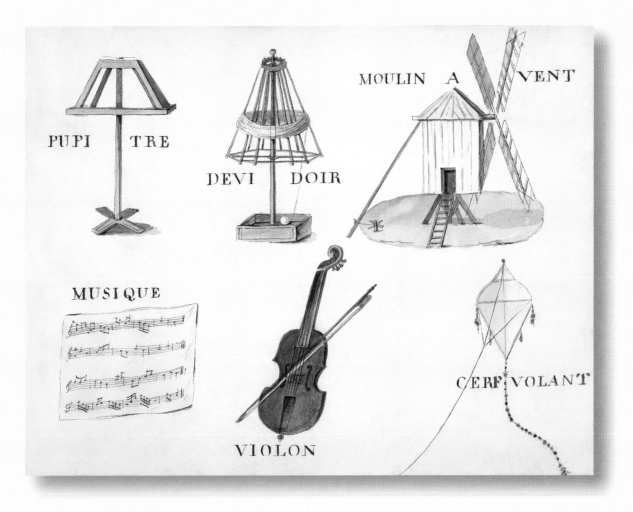

PUPI TRE

DEVI DOIR

MOULIN A VENT

MUSIQUE

VIOLON

CERF VOLANT

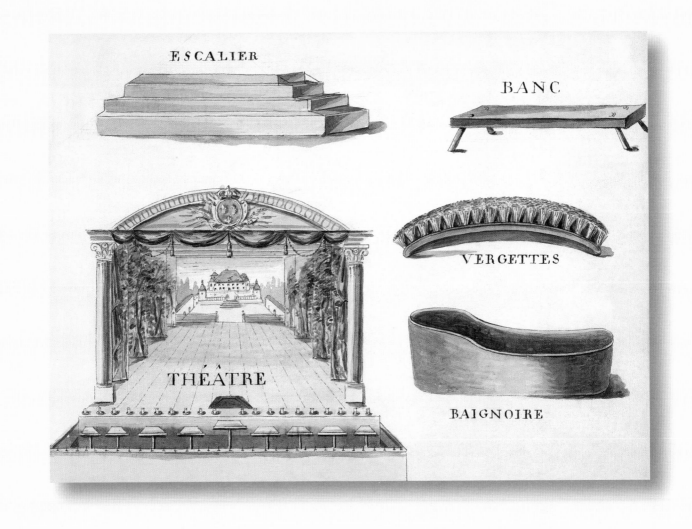

ESCALIER

BANC

VERGETTES

THÉÂTRE

BAIGNOIRE

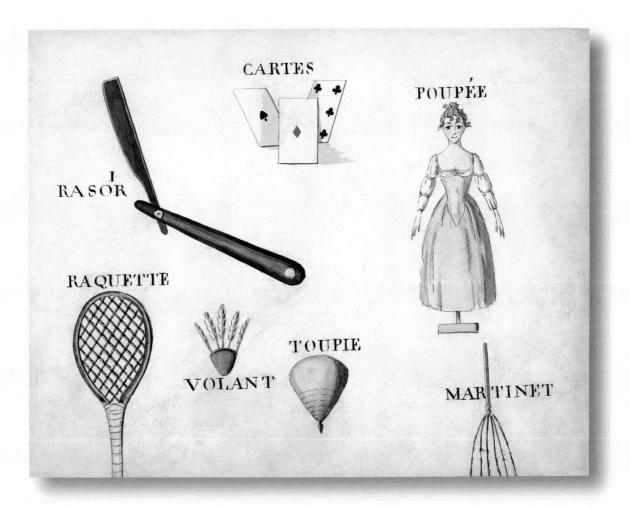

CARTES

POUPÉE

RASOR

RAQUETTE

VOLANT

TOUPIE

MARTINET

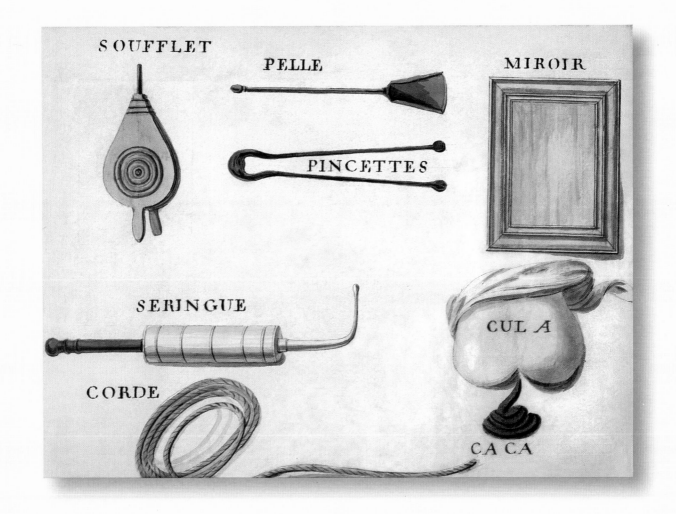

SOUFFLET

PELLE

MIROIR

PINCETTES

SERINGUE

CUL A

CORDE

CACA

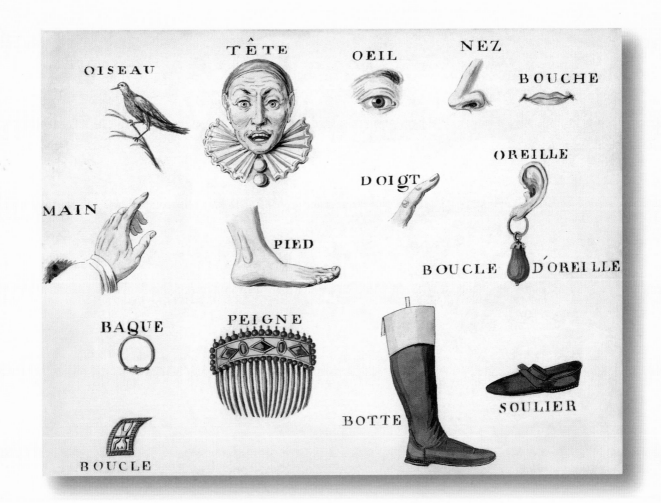

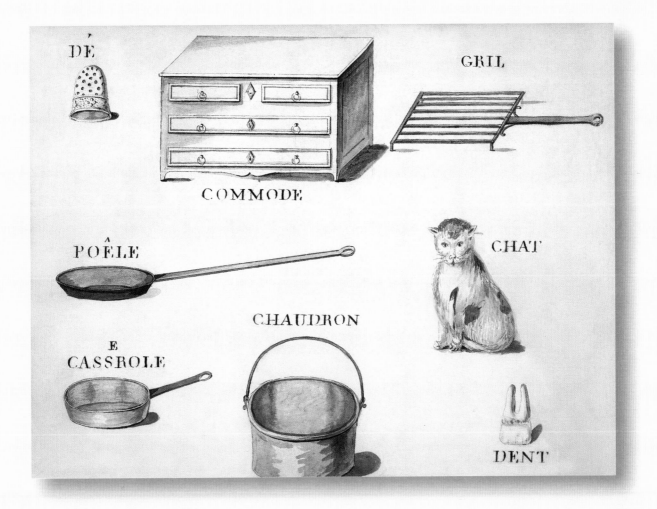

DÉ

COMMODE

GRIL

POÊLE

CHAT

E
CASSROLE

CHAUDRON

DENT

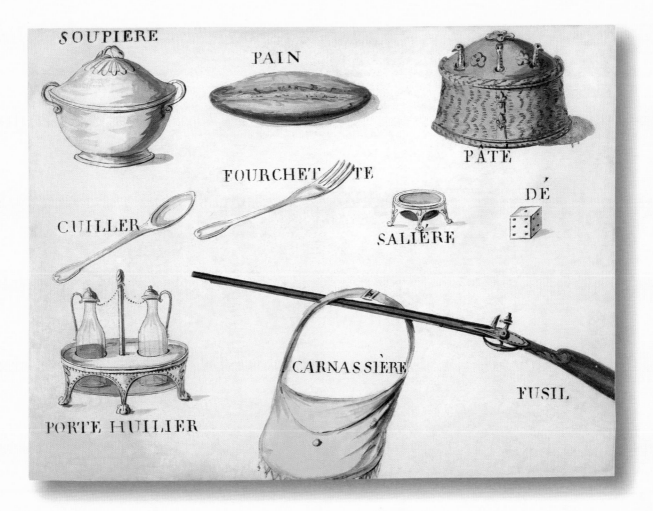

SOUPIERE

PAIN

PÂTE

FOURCHETTE

CUILLER

SALIÉRE

DÉ

PORTE HUILIER

CARNASSIÈRE

FUSIL

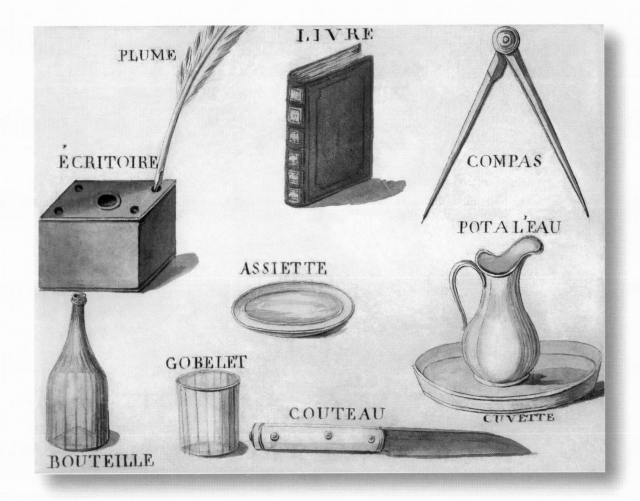

PLUME

LIVRE

COMPAS

ÉCRITOIRE

POT A L'EAU

ASSIETTE

GOBELET

COUTEAU

BOUTEILLE

CUVETTE

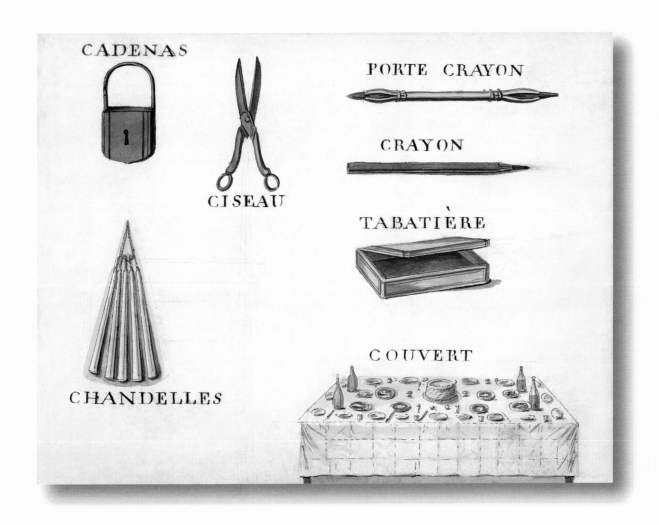

CADENAS

CISEAU

PORTE CRAYON

CRAYON

TABATIÈRE

CHANDELLES

COUVERT

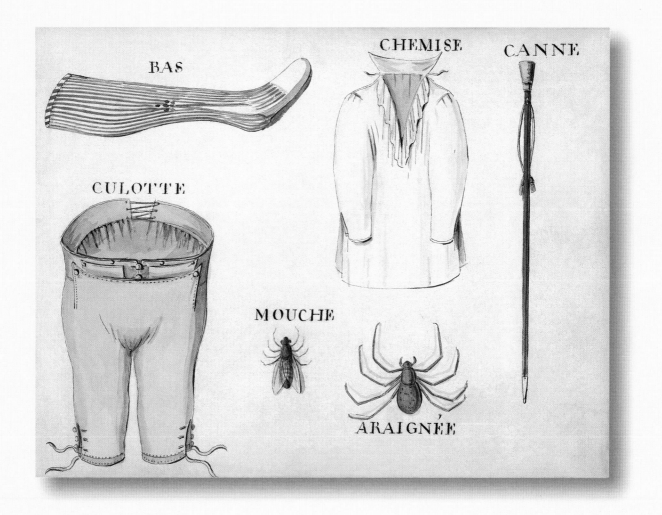

BAS

CHEMISE

CANNE

CULOTTE

MOUCHE

ARAIGNÉE

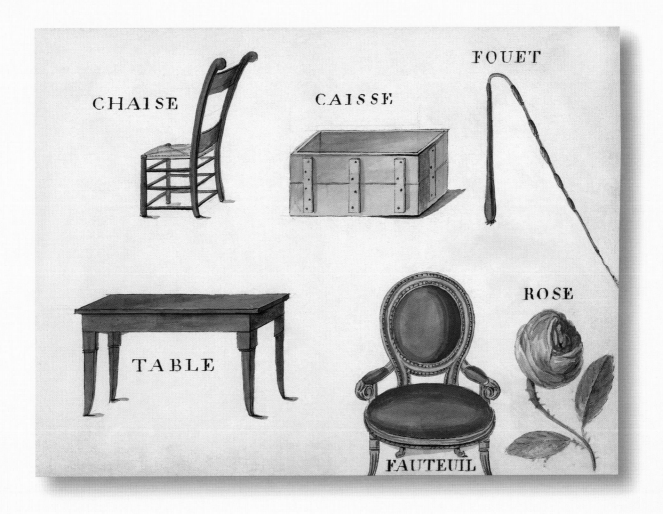

CHAISE

CAISSE

FOUET

ROSE

TABLE

FAUTEUIL

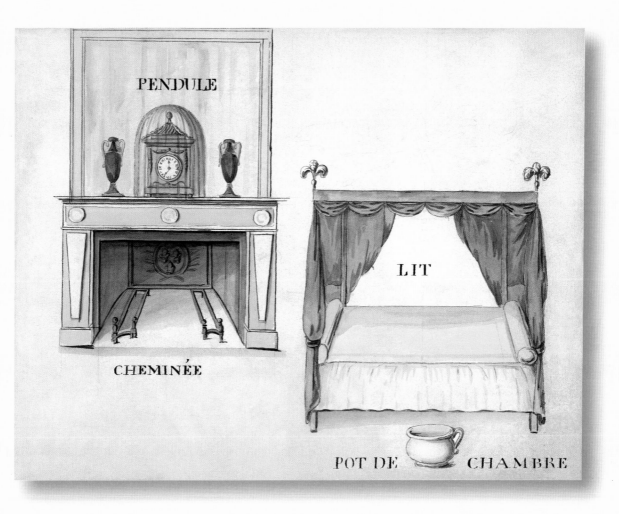

PENDULE

CHEMINÉE

LIT

POT DE CHAMBRE

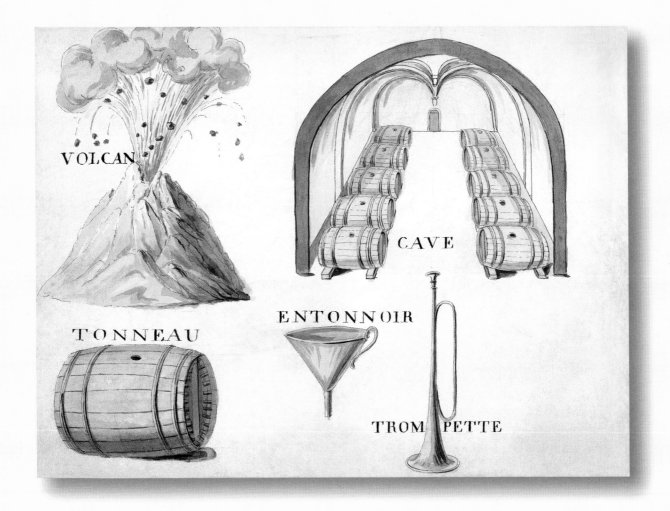

VOLCAN

CAVE

TONNEAU

ENTONNOIR

TROMPETTE

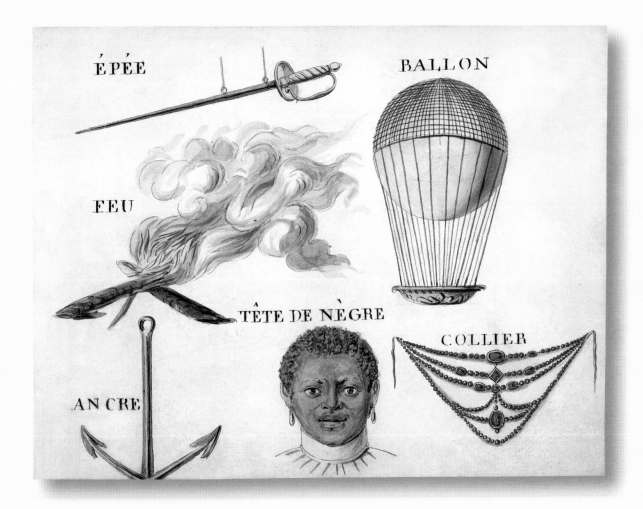

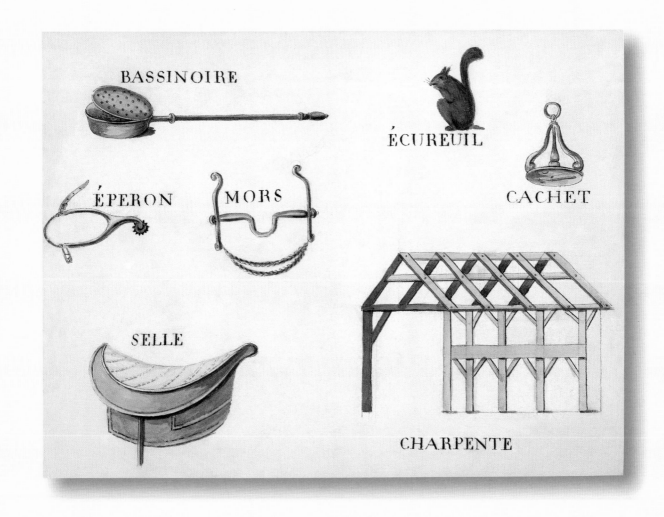

BASSINOIRE

ÉCUREUIL

CACHET

ÉPERON   MORS

SELLE

CHARPENTE

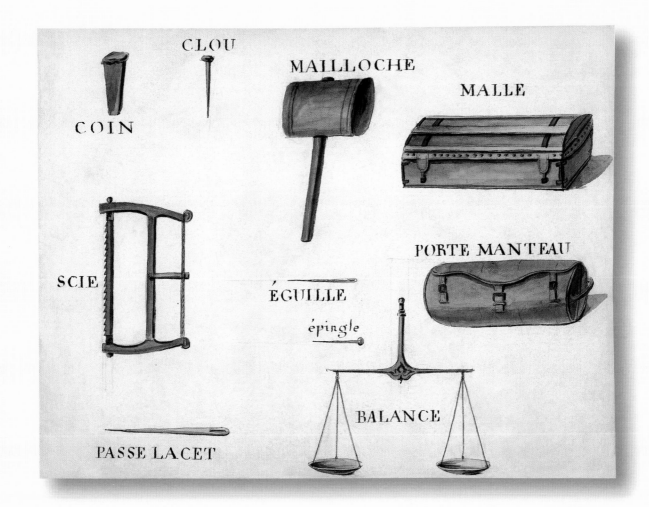

COIN

CLOU

MAILLOCHE

MALLE

SCIE

ÉGUILLE

épingle

PORTE MANTEAU

BALANCE

PASSE LACET

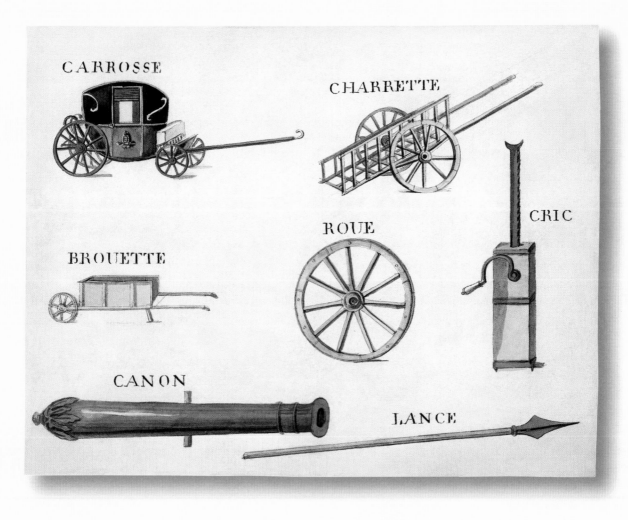

CARROSSE

CHARRETTE

CRIC

ROUE

BROUETTE

CANON

LANCE

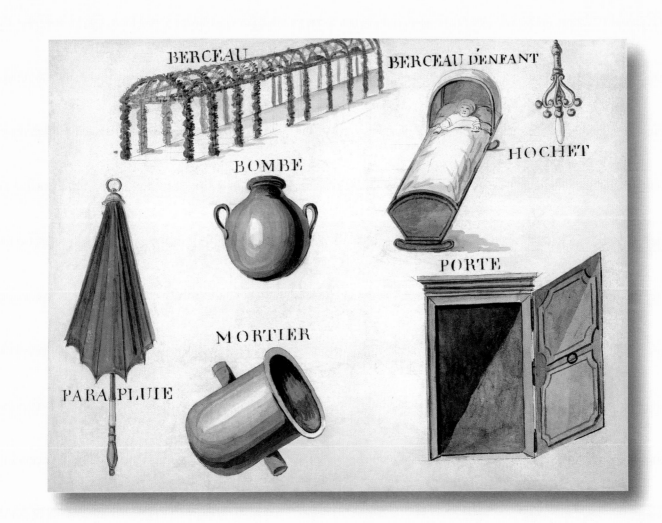

BERCEAU

BERCEAU D'ENFANT

HOCHET

BOMBE

PARAPLUIE

MORTIER

PORTE

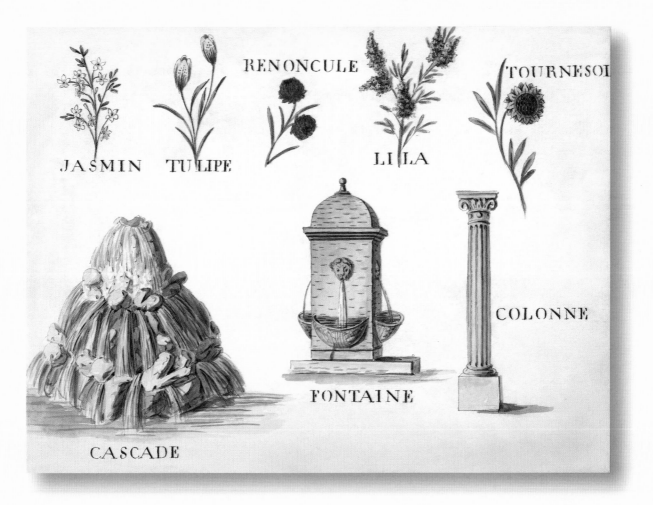

JASMIN   TULIPE   RENONCULE   LILA   TOURNESOL

CASCADE   FONTAINE   COLONNE

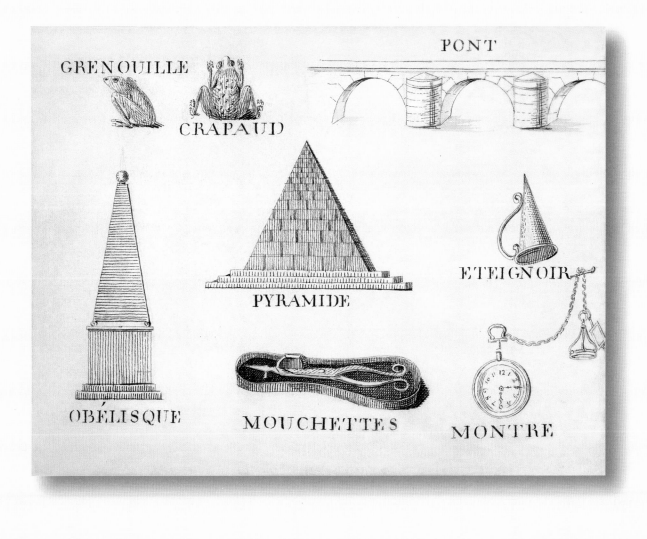

GRENOUILLE

CRAPAUD

PONT

OBÉLISQUE

PYRAMIDE

ETEIGNOIR

MOUCHETTES

MONTRE

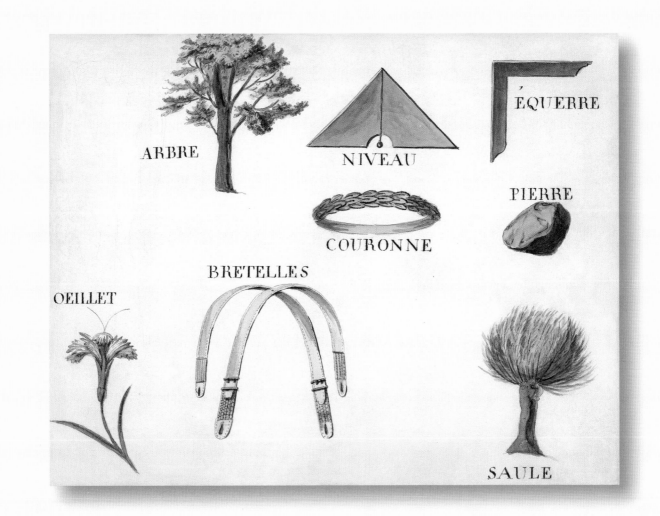

ARBRE

NIVEAU

L'ÉQUERRE

PIERRE

COURONNE

OEILLET

BRETELLES

SAULE

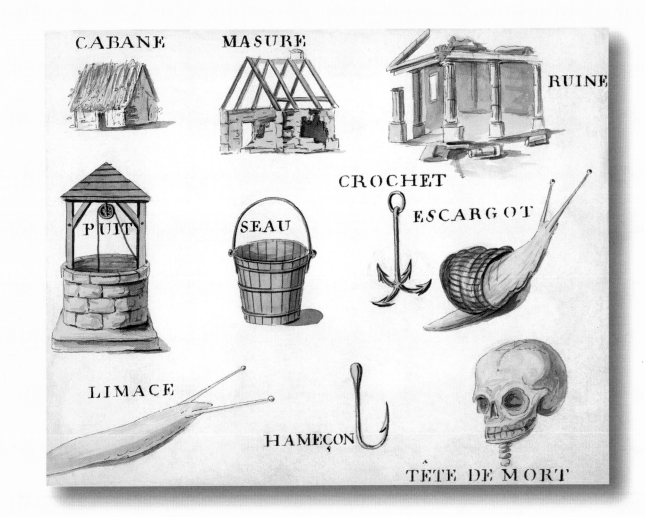

CABANE

MASURE

RUINE

CROCHET

PUIT

SEAU

ESCARGOT

LIMACE

HAMEÇON

TÊTE DE MORT

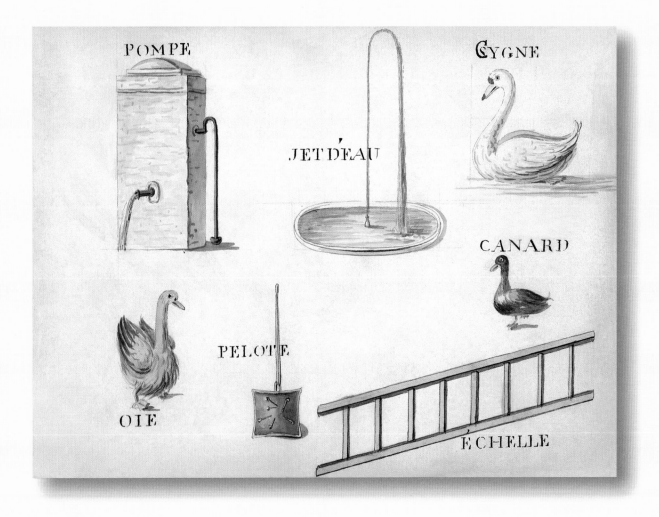

POMPE

JET D'EAU

CYGNE

CANARD

OIE

PELOTE

ÉCHELLE

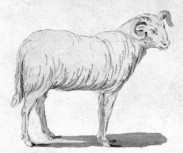

BELIER

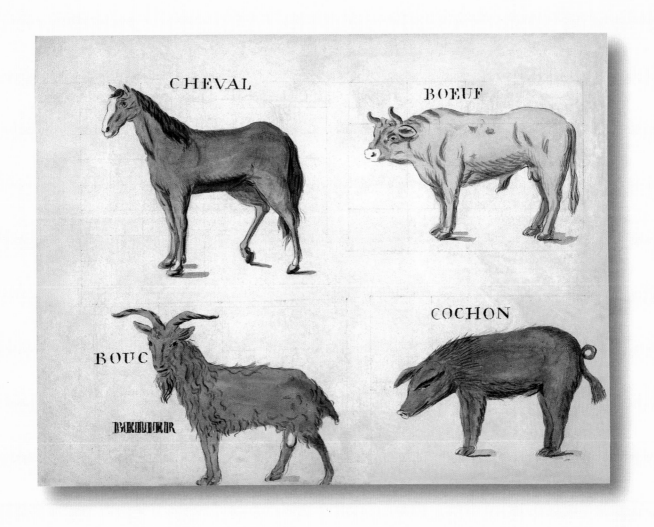

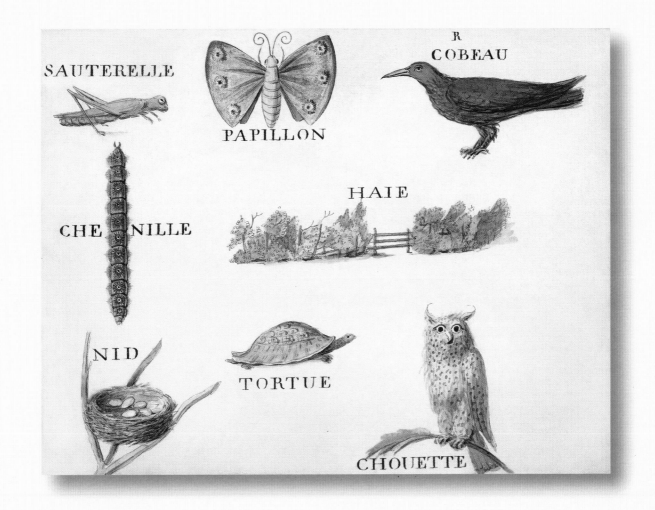

SAUTERELLE

PAPILLON

R
COBEAU

CHE NILLE

HAIE

NID

TORTUE

CHOUETTE

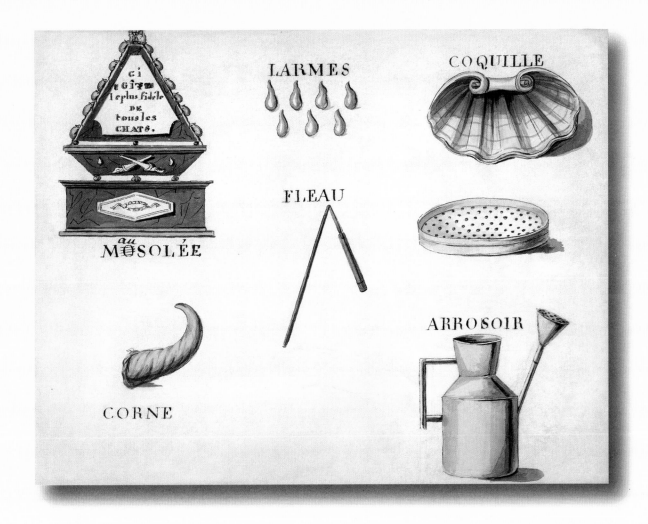

ci gît le plus fidèle de tous les CHATS.

au MOSOLÉE

LARMES

COQUILLE

FLEAU

CORNE

ARROSOIR

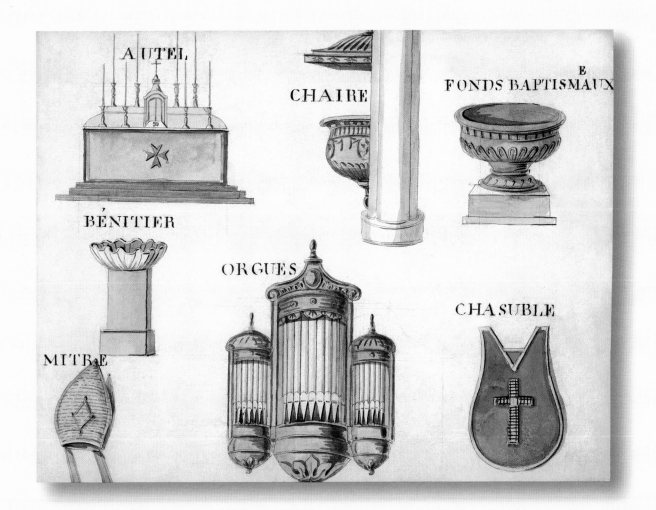

AUTEL

CHAIRE

FONDS BAPTISMAUX

BÉNITIER

ORGUES

CHASUBLE

MITRE

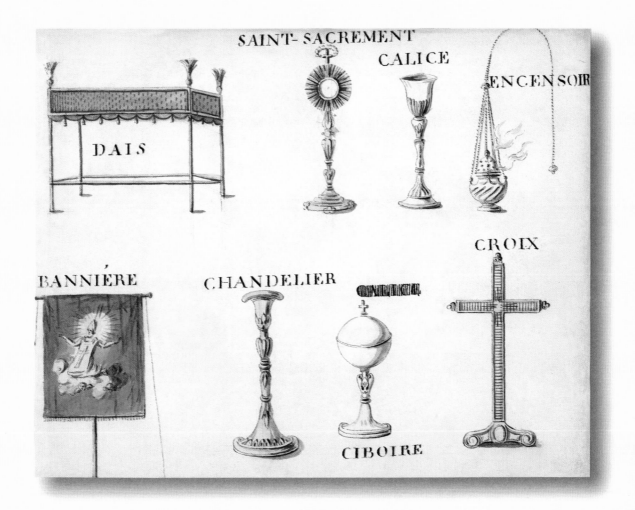

SAINT-SACREMENT

CALICE

ENCENSOIR

DAIS

CROIX

BANNIÉRE

CHANDELIER

CIBOIRE

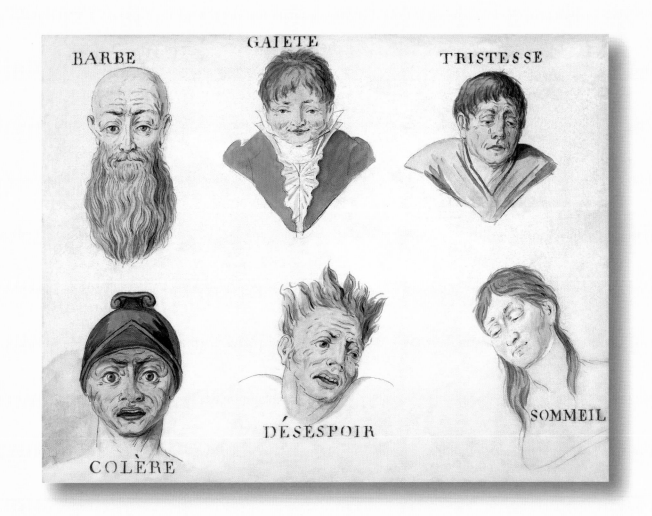

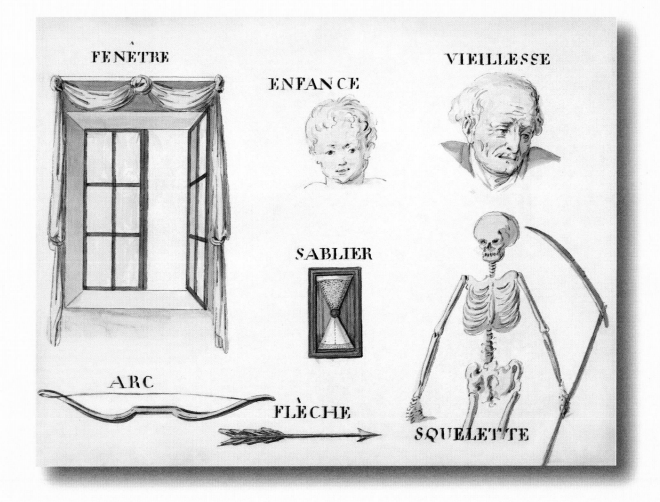

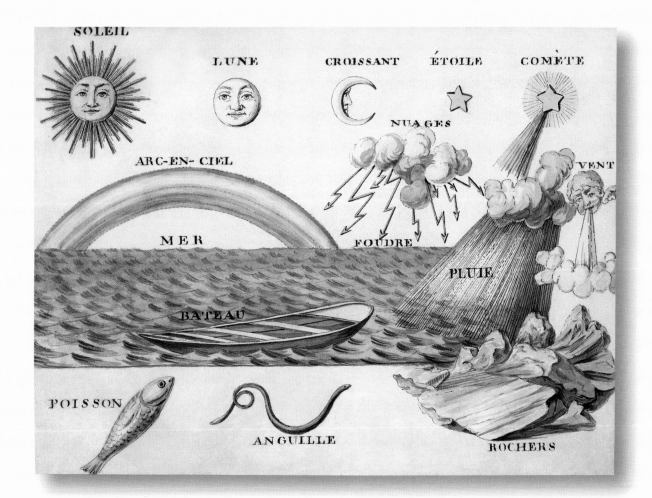

SOLEIL LUNE CROISSANT ÉTOILE COMÈTE

NUAGES

ARC-EN-CIEL VENT

MER FOUDRE

PLUIE

BATEAU

POISSON

ANGUILLE ROCHERS

CAYER D'INSTRUCTION
POUR ALFRED BOURDIER DE BEAUREGARD

The French entries (left column) are arranged alphabetically according to the first letters of the caption. Spelling mistakes and corrections have been preserved.

FRENCH	ENGLISH
A B C D E F G H / I J K L M N O P / Q R S T U V X Y / Z / Cayer d'instruction / pour Alfred Bourdier de Beauregard. / mon neveu, 1814 / Fait au chateau de Beauregard dans le courant de juin 1814 / par Arnaud, auteur du plan en Relief de la ville de Paris.	A B C D E F G H / I J K L M N O P / Q R S T U V X Y / Z / Instruction book / for Alfred Bourdier de Beauregard. / my nephew, 1814 / Made in the Beauregard country mansion in the course of June 1814 / by Arnaud, maker of the relief map of the city of Paris.
ANCRE	ANCHOR
ANGUILLE	EEL
ARAIGNÉE	SPIDER
ARBRE	TREE

FRENCH	ENGLISH
ARC	BOW
ARC-EN-CIEL	RAINBOW
ARROSOIR	WATERING POT
ASSIETTE	PLATE
AUBERGE	INN
AUTEL	ALTAR
avec l'amour toute la vie se passe comme un jour / avec l'amour toute la vie se passe comme un jour avec la […] / avec l'amour toute la vie […]	with love all life passes like a day / with love all life passes like a day with […] / with love all life […]
AVENUE	AVENUE OF TREES
BAGUE	RING
BAGUETTE	DRUM-STICK
BAIGNOIRE	BATHING-TUB
BALAI	BROOM
BALANCE	SCALES

FRENCH	ENGLISH
CHASUBLE	CHASUBLE
CHAT	CAT
CHATEAU / de Beaumont de Beauregard	COUNTRY MANSION / of Beaumont de Beauregard
CHAUDRON	CAULDRON
CHAUMIERE	COTTAGE
CHEMINÉE	CHIMNEYPIECE
CHEMISE	SHIRT
CHENILLE	CATERPILLAR
CHEVAL	HORSE
CHIFFRES / 1 2 3 4 5 6	NUMBERS / 1 2 3 4 5 6
CHOUETTE	OWL
ci / GÎTE / le plus fidéle / DE / tous les / CHATS. / MOAUSOLÉE	here / LIES / the most faithful / OF / all / CATS. / MAUSOLEUM
CISEAU	SCISSORS
CLEF	KEY

FRENCH	ENGLISH
CANNE	WALKING-STICK
CANON	CANNON
CARNASSIÈRE	GAME BAG
CARROSSE	COACH
CARTES	CARDS
CASCADE	WATERFALL
CASSEROLE	COPPER PAN
CAVE	WINE CELLAR
CERF VOLANT	KITE
CHAIRE	PULPIT
CHAISE	CHAIR
CHANDELIER	CANDLESTICK
CHANDELLES	CANDLES
CHAPEAU	HAT
CHARETTE	CART
CHARPENTE	TIMBER FRAME

FRENCH	ENGLISH
BOUCLE	SHOE-BUCKLE
BOUCLE D'OREILLE	EARRING
BOULE	BALL
BOUTEILLE	BOTTLE
BRETELLES	GALLOWSES
BROUETTE	WHEELBARROW
CABANE	HUT
CACHET	FOB
CADENAS	PADLOCK
CADRAN	DIAL
CADRAN SOLAIRE	SUN-DIAL
CAISSE	CHEST
CALICE	CHALICE
~~CALICE~~ / CIBOIRE	~~CHALICE~~ / CIBORIUM
CANARD	DUCK
CANIF	PENKNIFE

FRENCH	ENGLISH
BALLON	AIR-BALLOON
BANC	BENCH
BANNIÉRE	BANNER
BARBE	BEARD
BAS	STOCKING
BASSINOIRE	WARMING-PAN
BATEAU	BOAT
BELIER	RAM
BÉNITIER	HOLY WATER STOUP
BERCEAU	ARBOUR
BERCEAU D'ENFANT	CRADLE
BOEUF	OX
BOMBE	BOMB
BOTTE	BOOT
BOUC / ~~BELIER~~	GOAT / ~~RAM~~
BOUCHE	MOUTH

FRENCH	ENGLISH
CLOCHE	BELL
CLOCHER	BELL-TOWER
CLOU	NAIL
COCHON	PIG
COIN	WEDGE
COLÈRE	ANGER
COLLIER	NECKLACE
COLONNE	COLUMN
COMÈTE	COMET
COMMODE	CHEST OF DRAWERS
COMPAS	COMPASSES
COQUILLE	SHELL
COR DE CHASSE	HUNTING-HORN
CORBEAU	RAVEN
CORDE	ROPE
CORNE	HORN

FRENCH	ENGLISH
COURONNE	WREATH
COUTEAU	KNIFE
COUVERT	A SET UP TABLE
CRAPAUD	TOAD
CRAYON	PENCIL
CRIC	JACK
CROCHET	HOOK
CROISSANT	CRESCENT (MOON)
CROIX	CROSS
CUILLER	SPOON
CUL A / CACA	BOTTOM WITH / AH-AH
CULOTTE	KNEE BREECHES
CYGNE	SWAN
DAIS	CANOPY
DÉ	DICE
DÉ	THIMBLE

FRENCH	ENGLISH
DENT	TOOTH
DÉSESPOIR	DESPAIR
DEVIDOIR	SPINDLE
DOIGT	FINGER
DRAPEAU	FLAG
ÉCHELLE	LADDER
ÉCREVISSE	CRAYFISH
ÉCRITOIRE	INKWELL
ÉCUREUIL	SQUIRREL
ÉCURIE	STABLE
ÉGLISE	CHURCH
ÉGUILLE	NEEDLE
ENCENSOIR	CENSER
ENFANCE	CHILDHOOD
ENTONNOIR	FUNNEL
ÉPÉE	SWORD

FRENCH	ENGLISH
ÉPERON	SPUR
épingle	pin
ÉQUERRE	RULER
ESCALIER	STAIRS
ESCARGOT	SHELL-SNAIL
ETEIGNOIR	EXTINGUISHER
ÉTOILE	STAR
FAUTEUIL	ARM-CHAIR
FENÊTRE	WINDOW
FEU	FIRE
FLEAU	FLAIL
FLÈCHE	ARROW
FLÛTE	FLUTE
FONDS BAPTISMEAUX	BAPTISMAL FONT
FONTAINE	FOUNTAIN
FOUDRE	THUNDERBOLT

FRENCH	ENGLISH
FOUET	WHIP
FOURCHE	PITCH-FORK
FOURCHETTE	FORK
FUSIL	SPORTING GUN
GAIETE	GAIETY
GOBELET	GOBLET
GRANGE	BARN
GRATOIR	SCRAPER
GRENOUILLE	FROG
GRIL	GRIDIRON
GUITARE	GUITAR
HAIE	HEDGE
HAMEÇON	FISH-HOOK
HARPE	HARP
HOCHET	CORAL
HÔTEL	TOWN MANSION

FRENCH	ENGLISH
JARDIN	GARDEN
JASMIN	JASMINE
JET D'EAU	WATERSPOUT
LANCE	SPEAR
LARMES	TEARS
LETTRES / A B C D	LETTERS / A B C D
LILA	LILAC
LIMACE	SLUG
LIT	BED
LIVRE	BOOK
LUNE	MOON
LUNETTES	SPECTACLES
MAILLOCHE	WOODEN MALLET
MAIN	HAND
MAISON	TOWNHOUSE
MALLE	TRUNK

FRENCH	ENGLISH
MARTINET	MARTINET
MASURE	HOVEL
MER	SEA
MIROIR	MIRROR
MITRE	MITRE
MONTRE	WATCH
MORS	HORSE-BIT
MORTIER	MORTAR-PIECE
MOUCHE	FLY
MOUCHETTES	SNUFFERS
MOULIN A VENT	WINDMILL
MUSIQUE	SHEET MUSIC
NEZ	NOSE
NID	NEST
NIVEAU	LEVEL
NUAGES	CLOUDS

FRENCH	ENGLISH
OBÉLISQUE	OBELISK
OEIL	EYE
OEILLET	CARNATION
OEUF	EGG
OIE	GOOSE
OISEAU	BIRD
OREILLE	EAR
ORGUES	ORGAN
PAIN	BREAD
PALAIS	PALACE
PAPILLON	BUTTERFLY
PARAPLUIE	UMBRELLA
PASSE LACET	BODKIN
PÂTÉ	PIE
PEIGNE	COMB
PELLE	SHOVEL

FRENCH	ENGLISH
PELOTE	PINCUSHION
PENDULE	CLOCK
PIED	FOOT
PIERRE	STONE
PINCETTES	PINCERS
PLUIE	RAIN
PLUME	PEN
POÊLE	FRYING-PAN
POISSON	FISH
POMPE	PUMP
PONT	BRIDGE
PORT DE MER	SEA-PORT
PORTE	DOOR
PORTE CRAYON	PENCIL-CASE
PORTE FEUILLE	PORTFOLIO
PORTE HUILIER	OIL-CRUET SET

FRENCH	ENGLISH
PORTE MANTEAU	CLOAK BAG
POT A L'EAU / CUVETTE	WATER PITCHER / CHARGER
POT DE CHAMBRE	CHAMBER POT
POTENCE	GIBBET
POUPÉE	DOLL
PRISON	PRISON
PUIT	WELL
PUPITRE	LECTERN
PYRAMIDE	PYRAMID
RAQUETTE	RACKET
RASOIR	RAZOR
RAT	RAT
RENONCULE	CROWS-FOOT
ROCHERS	ROCKS
ROSE	ROSE
ROUE	WHEEL

FRENCH	ENGLISH
RUE	STREET
RUINE	RUINS
SABLIER	HOUR-GLASS
SABRE	SABRE
SAINT-SACREMENT	HOLY SACRAMENT
SALIÉRE	SALT-CELLAR
SAULE	WILLOW-TREE
SAUTERELLE	GRASSHOPPER
SAVON	SOAP
SCIE	SAW
SEAU	PAIL
SELLE	SADDLE
SERINGUE	SYRINGUE
SOLEIL	SUN
SOMMEIL	SLEEP
SOUFFLET	BELLOWS

FRENCH	ENGLISH
SOULIER	SHOE
SOUPIERE	TUREEN
SQUELETTE	SKELETON
SUCRE	SUGAR CONE
TABATIÈRE	SNUFF-BOX
TABLE	TABLE
TAMBOUR	DRUM
TÊTE	HEAD
TÊTE DE MORT	DEATH'S HEAD
TÊTE DE NÈGRE	HEAD OF A NEGRO
THÉÂTRE	THEATRE
TIMBALE	KETTLE-DRUM
TONNEAU	BARREL
TORTUE	TORTOISE
TOUPIE	WHIRL-GIGG
TOUR	TOWER

FRENCH	ENGLISH
TOURNESOL	SUNFLOWER
TRISTESSE	SADNESS
TROMPETTE	TRUMPET
TULIPE	TULIP
VAISSEAU	SAILING SHIP
VENT	WIND
VERGETTES	BRUSH
VIEILLESSE	OLD AGE
VILLAGE	VILLAGE
VILLE	TOWN
VIOLON	VIOLIN
VOLANT	SHUTTLECOCK
VOLCAN	VOLCANO

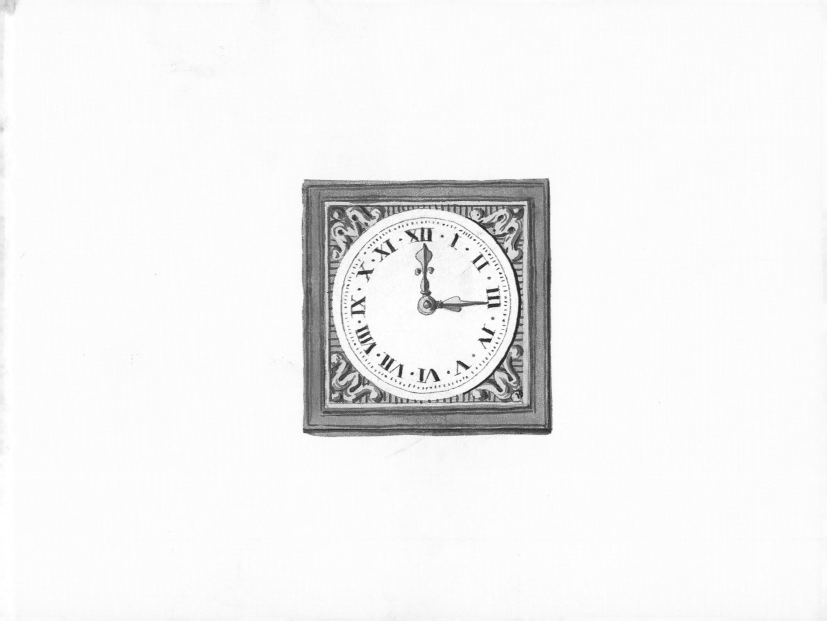

A B C D E F G H
I J K L M N O P
Q R S T U V X Y
Z A B C D E F G
H I J K L M N O
P Q R S T U V X